16.2.2024

Step by Step

Vegetarian

Step by Step

Vegetarian

Barbara Lowery

Bloomsbury Books
London

Page 2: Goat's Cheese and Sun-Dried Tomato Tartlets (p. 42). This tart makes a delicious starter or light luncheon dish served with a fresh salad and a glass of wine. The endpapers show the preparation for the tart.

This edition published in 1994 by
Bloomsbury Books
an imprint of
The Godfrey Cave Group
42 Bloomsbury Street, London. WC1B 3QJ
under license from
Harlaxton Publishing Limited

Harlaxton Publishing Limited
2 Avenue Road, Grantham, Lincolnshire, NG31 6TA
United Kingdom
A Member of the Weldon International Group of Companies

First Published in 1994

Publisher: Robin Burgess
Project Coordinator: Barbara Beckett
Designer: Rachel Rush
Editor: Alison Leach
Illustrator: Maggie Renvoize
Jacket photographer: Rodney Weidland
Inside photography: Andrew Elton
Food stylist: Barbara Lowery
Produced by Barbara Beckett Publishing
Colour Separation: G.A. Graphics, Stamford, UK
Printer: Imago, Singapore

British Library Cataloguing-in-Publication data.
A catalogue record for this book is available from the British Library

Title: Step by Step, VEGETARIAN
ISBN: 1 85471 397 3

Step by Step

Contents

Cook's Notes

Measurements

All spoon and cup measurements are level. Standard spoon and cup measures are used in all the recipes. I recommend using a graduated nest of measuring cups: 1 cup, ½ cup, ⅓ cup and ¼ cup. The graduated nest of spoons comprises 1 tablespoon, 1 teaspoon, ½ teaspoon and ¼ teaspoon. For liquids, use a standard litre or imperial pint measuring jug, which also shows cup measurements. As the metric and imperial equivalents given are not exact, only follow one system of measurement within the recipe.

Ovens should be preheated to the specified temperature. When cooking on the hob (stove plate), use medium heat where high, low or simmer are not specified. Microwave recipes have been tested using a 750 watt microwave oven.

Ingredients

Fresh **vegetables** and **fruits** should be used unless canned or dried are suggested. **Herb** quantities given are for fresh herbs; if fresh are unobtainable, use half the quantity of dried herbs. Use freshly ground black **pepper** whenever pepper is listed; use **salt** and pepper to individual taste. Use plain (all-purpose) **flour** unless otherwise stated. Fresh **ginger** should be used throughout; white granulated **sugar** is used unless stated otherwise and unsalted **butter** is used. **Eggs** used throughout the recipes are size 3 (60 g/2 oz). In the salad section on page 12 there are notes on **oils** and **vinegars**.

Mini Pumpkins with Fruity Couscous (p. 34) served with a leafy green salad studded with edible flowers. The couscous filling could also be used to stuff globe artichokes, baked onions, courgettes (baby marrows, zucchini) tomatoes or squash.

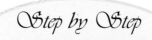

Introduction

Everyday meals would be extremely dull and uninteresting if it weren't for nature's rich bounty of vegetables. Full of vibrant colour, flavour and texture, vegetables make an important contribution to a healthy diet; they supply essential fibre, contain no fat and are satisfying to eat without supplying excess calories (kilojoules). However, as we know, vegetables on their own do not constitute a balanced diet. They contain insufficient of the body-building foods found in meat and fish and therefore need to be supplemented with a variety of foods containing essential vitamins, minerals, protein and a small amount of fats. Vegetarian meals need to be carefully planned to give a healthy balanced diet. This is not difficult. After all, George Bernard Shaw, who lived till he was 94, was a vegetarian.

The recipes in this book are not the usual vegetarian nut-meat loaf variety. They are designed for lacto-ovo vegetarians who eat dairy foods and eggs as well as plant foods, and for everyone who enjoys preparing and serving creative and delicious vegetable dishes. While most recipes in the book are suitable for casual everyday eating, some would star at the best dinner party. The freshest vegetables always have the best flavour, so people who grow their own are fortunate. For those of us who rely on produce markets or supermarkets for our supply, a well-trained eye will immediately identify freshness. Ideally, vegetables should be purchased at least three times a week and in hotter months, green leaf and salad vegetables should be purchased daily. Buy the vegetables that are in season; they are likely to have the most flavour.

The recipes are clearly set out, listing the ingredients in the order they are used. One of the most important things to do when trying a new recipe is to read the recipe very thoroughly before starting. Check that you have all the ingredients, and make an estimate of the amount of time needed.

There are step-by-step guides to the different cooking methods, such as poaching, braising and grilling (broiling). Many of the recipes are photographed in preparation stages to show a special technique as well as what the finished dish looks like and how to present it for the table. Detailed step-by-step drawings also illustrate how to stuff ravioli, bake a ricotta mould and making a roulade. There are handy hints, giving information such as how to measure out honey, cooking your own beans and cooking homemade pastry.

A glossary of cooking terms is on page 47 for you to look up any term that is unfamiliar. There is a list of recipes on page 5 for your reference. Be sure to read the information on measurements and ingredients on page 6.

Preparing vegetarian recipes is made easier if you have the following equipment. Most are standard items that you will already have in your kitchen.

A few well-sharpened **knives** are needed, including a small paring knife for peeling and cutting delicate vegetables; a large cook's knife for chopping hard vegetables like pumpkin;

a good **vegetable peeler**, preferably a brightly coloured one that will not be accidentally thrown out with the peelings.

A large wooden **chopping board** is required as well as a small one to be used only for cutting onion and garlic.You will need a few **flat wooden spoons**. These are more efficient to stir with than the traditional concave spoons. (It's a good idea to mark the handles of all wooden spoons with the words 'sweet' or 'savoury' and keep them for the purpose noted.)

Some smaller items: a **garlic crusher**; some pure bristle **pastry brushes**; a **grater** and a **colander (perforated strainer)**, preferably of stainless-steel; a stainless-steel **whisk** for whisking vinaigrette dressings; a **salad drier**; a **sieve**; plastic or nylon **scrapers**.

A stainless-steel **baking dish** is a good investment as it can be cleaned easily. A **food processor**, comprising a bowl with metal blade, and slicing and grating discs. A **steamer** and **wok** are ideal for cooking vegetables in. A **microwave oven** will speed up many cooking processes and is now standard equipment in many kitchens.

Storage of Vegetables

Once purchased, vegetables must be stored properly, whether it's for only a day or for a week. Before storing, take them out of the polythene shopping bags or wrapping. It's best to wash vegetables just before using. Remove outer leaves or stems of spinach, broccoli, leeks, fennel and cabbage and store the vegetables in the crisper of the refrigerator. Leave husks and silk on sweetcorn during storage. Root vegetables such as carrots, parsnips, beetroot and turnips, and hard vegetables like potatoes, onions and pumpkin, should be stored in a cool, dark, dry well-ventilated place. Potatoes in particular are affected by light; they can turn green, appear bitter in flavour and can even cause illness.

Pod vegetables including all types of peas and beans should be stored unshelled in a paper bag in the vegetable crisper and shelled or sliced just before cooking. Store dried peas, beans and lentils in glass screw-topped jars. Kept in a cool, dry, dark place. These dried vegetables will keep for months.

Drying Salad Leaves

| *Wash the leaves in a bowl of very cold water.* | *If you have a salad drier, place the leaves in the basket.* | *Close the lid and spin.* | *Alternatively, dry the leaves in a clean tea-towel (dish cloth) and pat dry.* |

Oils and Vinegars

Always cook with the best quality olive oil you can afford; many a cook is judged on the oil they choose. For flavour and nutritional value, cholesterol-free, mono-unsaturated olive oil cannot be surpassed. Various grades of olive oil are available to suit different cooking needs.

Extra virgin is the ultimate olive oil. It's the first pressing of best quality barely ripe olives, done without applying heat so natural anti-oxidants are preserved. Perfect in taste and odour, this oil has an intense fruity flavour and shows the character of the growing region, just as wine does. By law, olives used for this oil must be pressed within 72 hours of harvesting. The magical flavour of olive oil is most evident when it's consumed `raw' in salad dressings and when drizzled over cooked foods.

Virgin olive oil is the second pressing of the olives and, like extra virgin oil, is used sparingly as it also is rich in flavour.

Pure olive oil is lighter and, being a well-refined oil with the addition of virgin oil, it has a more subtle flavour. It's an ideal oil for sautéing foods in, and for using in mayonnaise, vegetable sauces and casseroles.

Light olive oil is very well-refined oil and it's bland in flavour. It has been designed to meet consumer demand for 'light' foods and is therefore suitable for light vinaigrette dressings, for sautéing, for stir-frying and for use in cake and muffins. It is also the recommended oil for deep-frying as it tolerates a higher temperature than most others without breaking down. The food is therefore sealed immediately it comes into contact with the oil and absorbes less fat. Contrary to popular belief, all oils contain the same number of calories (kilojoules).

Peanut oil is excellent for stir-frying and for imparting a subtle nutty flavour to Oriental-style dressings.

Sesame oil has a distinctive concentrated sesame flavour that enhances Oriental-style dressings and stir-fried dishes.

Vinegar plays an important role in dressings and it pays to use a top quality product. While white wine (fermented) vinegar is most commonly used, flavoured vinegars are becoming increasingly popular. Herb and spices used to flavour vinegars include dill, tarragon, rosemary and chilli. Cider vinegar is often used in Oriental-style dressings, and raspberry and other fruit-flavoured vinegars are appearing in well-dressed salads.

Balsamic vinegar comes from Modena in Italy and is made from unfermented Trebbiano grapes, a variety used for making white wine. Deep in colour, balsamic vinegar has a wonderful flavour. It is expensive, but a little goes a long way. Use it sparingly in dressings and sprinkled over steamed vegetables.

Tomato and Olive Fettuccine.(p. 18) Penne, pasta spirals, bow ties, or spaghetti may be used in place of fettuccine.

Step by Step

Salads

A bright colourful salad, lovingly prepared from the freshest vegetables in season, should delight the eye, nose and palate. With an ever-increasing variety of vegetables available, and ingredients and dressings drawn from cuisines around the world, there is little excuse for mundane salads. They can be simple, casual or more elaborate, depending on the occasion. When presented raw and unpeeled in salads, vegetables usually offer maximum nutritional value as the valuable nutrients that lie just beneath the skin are eaten. Leafy green vegetables should be washed and dried in a salad spin drier or basket which removes moisture without bruising fragile leaves. When dry, place them in a sealed polythene bag or airtight container in the refrigerator. Most dressings can be prepared in advance to allow flavours to blend, but the salad itself should be assembled just prior to serving. This of course does not apply to root vegetables or ingredients that need to be marinated in the dressing. Remember that green vegetables discolour quickly when combined with a vinaigrette, so add the dressing just before serving. For the perfect salad, start with the freshest, most colourful vegetables in season, add a tantalizing dressing and enjoy!

Grated Beetroot Salad

This delicious salad has a refreshing sweet-and-sour flavour. Beetroot juice stains the skin, so it's a good idea to wear new rubber gloves when peeling and grating it.

6 small raw beetroot, coarsely grated
90 g/3 oz/½ cup sultanas (golden raisins)
4 spring onions, sliced
1 white onion, finely sliced
60 g/2 oz/½ cup chopped walnuts
Finely grated peel of 1 orange

VINAIGRETTE
4 tablespoons light olive oil
1 tablespoon strained orange juice
1 teaspoon white vinegar
Salt and pepper

Watercress or green salad leaves, to garnish

Place the salad ingredients in a bowl and mix to combine. Whisk the vinaigrette ingredients together in a small bowl, pour over the salad and toss. Cover and chill the salad lightly before serving. Serve garnished with watercress or green salad leaves.
Serves 4–6

Bean and Artichoke Salad

Legumes are rich in protein and fibre, but low in cholesterol and fat. Use canned red kidney and lima beans or, if you have time, it's far more economical to cook dried beans. Cook extra quantities and freeze some for up to 6 months.

375 g/13 oz French (green) beans
250 g/9 oz/1½ cups cooked red kidney beans
250 g/9 oz/1½ cups cooked lima beans
1 red onion, sliced
400 g/14 oz can artichoke hearts, drained
12 cherry tomatoes

VINAIGRETTE
3 tablespoons olive oil
1 tablespoon lemon juice
1 garlic clove, crushed
1 teaspoon chopped thyme
Salt and pepper

Cut the French beans in half and cook in boiling water until tender but still firm. Drain and refresh under cold running water. Drain again. Place French, kidney and lima beans in a bowl with the onion, artichoke hearts and tomatoes. Whisk the vinaigrette ingredients in a small bowl and pour over the salad ingredients. Toss well and leave the salad to stand for 30 minutes before serving.

Serves 6

Cooking Dried Beans. *Soak dried kidney and lima beans separately in cold water overnight, allowing 750 ml/1¼ pints/3 cups of water to each 175g/6 oz/1 cup of beans. Discard the soaking water and replace with the same quantity of fresh water. Boil the beans rapidly in unsalted water for 10 minutes; then reduce the heat and keep the water just boiling until the beans are tender (the time will vary, depending on the type of bean). Beans may also be cooked in half the time in the microwave oven.*

Making Beetroot Salad

If you want to avoid stained hands, put on rubber gloves.

Peel and grate the beetroot.

Place the salad ingredients in a bowl and mix.

Whisk the vinaigrette ingredients together.

Sweet Potato and Avocado Salad

Golden sweet potato is delicious when teamed with avocado and a spicy mayonnaise. This colourful, nutritious salad is best served at room temperature.

575 g/1¼ lb sweet potatoes (kumera)
Squeeze of lemon juice

DRESSING
125 ml/4 fl oz/ ½ cup mayonnaise
125 ml/4 fl oz / ½ cup plain yoghurt
2 teaspoons clear honey, warmed (p. 27)

½ teaspoon curry powder
45 g/1½ oz/¼ cup chopped spring onions (scallions)
1 avocado, sliced
30 g/1 oz/¼ cup flaked (slivered) almonds, toasted

Lemon wedges, to garnish

Cut the sweet potato into 2.5 cm/1 inch cubes and cook in boiling water with lemon juice. Cook until tender, but slightly firm. Drain well, leave to cool and place in a serving dish. Mix the mayonnaise, yoghurt, honey and curry powder and spoon over the sweet potato. Scatter with the spring onions, avocado and almonds. Serve garnished with lemon wedges.
Serves 4

Fresh Tomato Sauce

750 g/1¾ lb ripe tomatoes, peeled
2 tablespoons olive oil
1 onion, finely chopped
1 garlic clove, crushed

250 ml/8 fl oz/1 cup tomato juice
Pinch of sugar
Salt and pepper

Cut the tomatoes in half and squeeze gently to release the seeds. Chop the tomatoes finely. Heat the oil in a large pan and cook the onion and garlic gently until soft but not brown. Add the tomatoes, tomato juice, sugar, salt and pepper. Simmer the sauce, uncovered, for 10 minutes.

Peeling Tomatoes

Put the tomatoes into a bowl and pour boiling water over them.	*Remove after several minutes and place under cold running water.*	*Make a slit in the skin at the base.*	*Slip the skin off.*
1	2	3	4

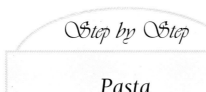

Step by Step

Pasta

Pasta is made from wheat flour or durum semolina and water, sometimes with the addition of eggs. It is available in a wonderful variety of shapes, sizes and colours. A popular food in many countries, it marries well with other ingredients and can be served hot or cold. It's also convenient to buy in dried form, stores easily in a cool dark place, takes a short time to cook and is inexpensive.

'Instant' lasagne sheets that require no preliminary cooking are particularly convenient. Fresh pasta can be purchased in supermarkets. If you are using fresh pasta in a recipe calling for dried pasta, you will need to double the quantity. When cooking pasta, use plenty of briskly boiling salted water.

Pasta should be added to the water slowly and the water returned to the boil as quickly as possible. It should also be stirred frequently and some cooks recommend adding a few drops of olive oil to the water to keep the pieces separate while cooking.

Salt is necessary to flavour pasta otherwise it is bland and dull. Allow 4 litres/7 pints/4¼ quarts of water and 2 tablespoons of salt for every 500 g/18 oz of pasta.

Cook pasta for the minimum time recommended on the pack, then sample a small piece to see if it is cooked. It should be firm in the centre and slightly resistant to the bite. This is described in Italian as *al dente*.

Preparing ravioli for Pumpkin Ravioli with Sun-Dried Tomatoes (p. 16). Don't be tempted to overdo the pumpkin filling—more than a teaspoonful could expand enough to burst the won ton wrappers during cooking.

Pumpkin Ravioli with Sun-Dried Tomatoes

This superb ravioli makes a wonderful entrée or main course for luncheon and is unbelievably easy, providing you know the secret. The ravioli is made in minutes from won ton wrappers (small pastry squares) available from chill cabinets of major supermarkets or Oriental stores. Simply follow the directions and no one will suspect that you didn't spend hours making your own pasta! You can buy sun-dried tomatoes in oil. Use this oil in vinaigrette dressings or for drizzling over steamed vegetables.

500 g/18 oz butternut pumpkin	1 egg, beaten
30 g/1 oz/¼ cup grated Parmesan cheese	3 tablespoons virgin olive oil
Salt and pepper	12–18 sun-dried tomatoes
250 g/8 oz packet won ton wrappers	2 tablespoons chopped basil

Cook or microwave the pumpkin until just tender. Drain well and mash. For this recipe the pumpkin needs to be fairly dry. Stir the Parmesan cheese into the hot pumpkin, add salt and pepper and leave the mixture to cool. To make the ravioli, arrange four won ton wrappers on a board, brush edges lightly with the egg, then place one heaped teaspoon of pumpkin on each wrapper. Top each with a second wrapper, pressing the edges firmly together to secure. Cut the ravioli into circles using a 7.5 cm/3 inch biscuit (cookie) cutter. Repeat this process until all the pumpkin is used. Bring a large pan of salted water to the boil and cook the ravioli for about 2–3 minutes, until *al dente*. Remove very carefully with a slotted spoon and drain. (Ravioli should be cooked in several batches.) Place the oil in a clean pan, add the ravioli, dried tomatoes and basil and swirl the pan very gently until the ravioli is coated with oil. Serve immediately.
Serves 4

Stuffing Ravioli

Mash and season the pumpkin mixture.	Brush the edges of the won ton wrappers with egg.	Top each one with a second wrapper and press edges firmly to secure.	Cut ravioli into circles with a biscuit (cookie) cutter.

Pumpkin Ravioli with Sun-Dried Tomatoes. Serve three ravioli per person as a starter or more as a main meal.

Some of the ingredients for Tomato and Olive Fettuccine. If a more subtle lemon peel flavour is desired, lemon shreds may be blanched quickly and added to the tomato mixture.

Tomato and Olive Fettuccine

Lemon peel adds an unusual flavour and fragrance to this delicious pasta sauce.

1 lemon

3 tomatoes, peeled, seeded and diced

1 garlic clove, crushed

2 tablespoons virgin olive oil

1 tablespoons chopped basil

1 tablespoon chopped oregano

75 g/2½ oz/½ cup sliced black olives

Pepper

500 g/18 oz dried fettuccini or 1 kg/2¼ lb fresh
   fettuccine

Grated Parmesan cheese, to serve

Remove thin strips of peel from the lemon using a vegetable peeler and cut the strips into very fine shreds. Place the peel in a bowl with the tomatoes, garlic, olive oil, basil, oregano, olives and pepper. Cook the fettuccine in plenty of boiling salted water until *al dente* and drain. Add the tomato mixture and toss to combine. Serve the pasta immediately, topped with grated Parmesan cheese.

Serves 4

Cutting Vegetables

To dice or cube vegetables, cut into rectangles of the thickness required.	*Cut the rectangles into dice.*	*For julienne strips, cut vegetables into thin slices:*	*Stack several slices together and slice into matchstick size.*

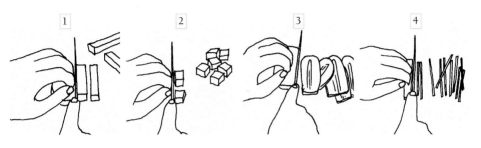

Using Soy Sauce. *Light soy sauce, which contains about half the salt of regular soy sauce, is becoming increasingly popular. If it is unavailable, dilute regular soy sauce with an equal quantity of water.*

Satay Noodles with Vegetables

Garam masala, an essential ingredient in this recipe, is an aromatic spice mixture available commercially. However, a homemade version is far fresher and superior in taste. Consult a good Indian cook book for a recipe and store the spice blend in a screw-topped jar in the refrigerator.

2 tablespoons peanut oil
1 garlic clove, crushed
1 teaspoon grated fresh root ginger
90 g/3 oz/⅓ cup crunchy peanut butter
2 teaspoons garam masala
1 tablespoon soy sauce

1 teaspoon sesame oil
250 g/9 oz fine egg noodles
150 g/5 oz/2 cups broccoli florets, blanched
60 g/2 oz/1 cup mung bean sprouts
1 tablespoon chopped coriander (cilantro)
2 spring onions (scallions), finely sliced

Heat the oil in a small pan and cook the garlic and ginger over a low heat for 30 seconds. Stir in the peanut butter, garam masala, soy sauce and sesame oil. Cook the noodles in plenty of boiling salted water in a large pan until *al dente* and drain. Return the noodles to the pan and stir in the peanut butter mixture. Add the broccoli, sprouts, coriander and spring onions and toss the ingredients gently to heat through.
Serves 4

Cook's Note: *Use a dry pastry brush to remove all lemon peel from a grater.*

Step by Step

Stir-Frying

This is one of the most healthy and nutritious methods of cooking vegetables. As virtually no water is used, nutrients, colour and texture of vegetables are retained. Traditionally a wok is used, but a large shallow pan will give equally good results once the stir-frying technique is mastered.

The procedure is quick and simple, therefore all the ingredients should be prepared before you start the cooking. Vegetables need to be cut to a uniform size so that they cook evenly. Generally the wok is heated, then a minimum amount of peanut or olive oil is added and flavoured if liked with garlic, ginger, spices or chilli. Cook the firm vegetables first, for one or two minutes, then the softer vegetables such as broccoli, cauliflower and beans. Add the more fragile vegetables like shredded cabbage, mangetouts (snow peas) and bean sprouts last. If liked, the vegetables can be covered for the last minute or two to steam slightly when all the vegetables should be cooked evenly. Seasonings like soy sauce and herbs should be added just before serving.

Stir-Fried Mushrooms with Polenta Blinis

Ideally, gather a variety of fresh mushrooms for this easy stir-fried dish. Button, field, straw, oyster or shiitake mushrooms provide a contrast in colour and flavour, while wild ceps or morels would add a truly exotic flavour.

BLINIS
125 g/4 oz/1 cup plain (all-purpose) flour
½ teaspoon salt
60 g/2 oz/½ cup fine ground polenta (cornmeal)
1 teaspoon dried yeast
1 teaspoon caster (superfine) sugar
2 eggs, separated
1 tablespoon olive oil

250 ml/8 fl oz/1 cup warm milk

MUSHROOMS
3 tablespoons olive oil
1 garlic clove, finely chopped
500 g/18 oz assorted mushrooms
1 tablespoon chopped Italian (flat-leaf) parsley

To make the blinis, sift the flour and salt into a bowl, add the polenta, yeast and sugar. Make a well in the centre and add the egg yolks, oil and half of the milk. Beat with a wooden spoon to make a thick batter and add the remaining milk gradually. Cover and leave the batter to stand for 1 hour. Beat the egg whites until stiff but not rocky and fold into the batter. Brush a hot frying pan (skillet) with olive oil and pour 2 tablespoons of batter into the pan. Cook the blinis over a moderate heat until bubbles appear on the surface, then turn them and cook until the base is golden brown.

Tofu Stir-Fry (p. 22). Use a stainless steel knife for cutting tofu to prevent discoloration. Have all ingredients prepared and assembled before you begin to cook. If beans are too large, cut them in half.

To cook the mushrooms, heat the oil in a pan and cook garlic gently for 30 seconds. Add the mushrooms and stir-fry until tender. Pile the mushrooms on to warm blinis and sprinkle with the parsley.
Serves 4

Making Blinis

Make a well in the polenta. Add egg yolks, oil and half the milk.	*Beat the batter and add remaining milk. Fold in beaten egg whites.*	*Pour 2 tablespoons of batter into a greased pan.*	*When heat bubbles appear on the surface flip the blini over.*

Tofu Stir-Fry

Tofu (also known as bean curd) is of Japanese origin. It is the most important by-product of the nutritious soya bean as it's rich in protein and low in fat. Fresh tofu is available in 'firm' or 'silken' form from the chill cabinets at most supermarkets and health food stores. Firm tofu can be cut into cubes, while silken tofu is often blended with other ingredients to make drinks, dressings and soups. Whatever the style, tofu has the ability to absorb other flavours quickly.

2 tablespoons peanut oil

1 garlic clove, finely chopped

1 teaspoon finely chopped ginger root

1 red onion, sliced

125g/4 oz/1 cup thinly sliced celery

1 red pepper (capsicum, bell pepper), sliced

1 carrot, cut into julienne strips

125 g/4 oz French (green) beans, blanched

75g/2½ oz/1 cup broccoli florets, blanched

2 tablespoons light soy sauce

3 tablespoons dry sherry

1 teaspoon caster (superfine) sugar

125 g/4 oz mangetout (snow peas)

250 g/9 oz firm tofu, cubed

Steamed or boiled rice, to serve

Heat the oil in a wok or large frying pan (skillet), add the garlic, ginger and onion and stir-fry over a high heat for 1 minute. Add the celery, pepper, carrot, beans and broccoli and stir-fry for 3 minutes. Mix the soy sauce, sherry and sugar together in a bowl and add to the vegetables with the mangetout and tofu. Stir-fry for a further 2 minutes and serve immediately with steamed or boiled rice.

Serves 2

Vegetable Crisps

Potato crisps have always been a popular food, but did you know that other vegetables also make delicious crisps? Good results depend on the vegetables being cut into wafer-thin slices. You can use the metal slicing blade of a food processor to do this quickly. Vegetable crisps can be made beforehand and stored in an airtight container.

Parsnips

Sweet potatoes

Celeriac

Jerusalem artichokes

Raw beetroot

Peanut or light olive oil for frying

Salt, to serve

Cut the peeled vegetables into 1 mm/¹⁄₁₆ inch slices. The slices of celeriac and Jerusalem artichoke should be placed in a bowl of water with a squeeze of lemon juice to prevent discolouring. Pat all the sliced vegetables dry before frying, as any moisture present will prevent them from browning evenly. Heat the oil in a large pan and deep-fry the vegetable slices a few at a time until pale golden brown. Drain on paper towels and sprinkle with salt just before serving.

Above: Tofu Stir-Fry ready to serve. Remember to rinse or wipe the wok out thoroughly after use. If the wok is made from tempered steel, dry it over a low heat, then rub very lightly with oil to prevent rusting.

Overleaf: Mediterranean Vegetables (p. 39). Brightly coloured vegetables ready for brushing with thyme and garlic-scented olive oil and baking in the oven.

Microwaving

In these busy times, most people consider a microwave an essential. You can cook meals in it quickly and efficiently, you can reheat food without dehydrating it and you can thaw food in minutes. Unlike the conventional oven, the microwave oven doesn't heat the kitchen while in use.

Most vegetables can be cooked to perfection in a microwave oven. Along with steaming and stir-frying, this cooking method has the added advantage of retaining more of the vitamin C content, as well as the fresh flavour and natural colour of the vegetables. When cooking in the microwave, check the food before the end of the cooking time. If it is cooked already, take it out of the microwave. Overcooking dries out vegetables and makes them tough.

When microwaving vegetables whole, pierce the skin with a skewer or fork to allow steam to escape. As most vegetables contain water, when microwaving them, you need to add only enough to create steam. If the food has been covered during microwaving, be careful not to get burned by the steam when removing the clingfilm (plastic wrap) or lid. Always lift the lid, or peel back the clingfilm, from the side of the dish furthest away from you. Allow vegetables to stand for 3-4 minutes after cooking.

Don't add salt when microwaving vegetables as it draws moisture and dehydrates them.

Like conventional ovens, the different models of microwave vary considerably in their behaviour. Consult the manufacturer's handbook if you are not sure how your model works.

Recipes in this book have been tested in a 750 watt microwave with a turntable. If your microwave has a lower output (wattage), increase the cooking times slightly. Cooking times given are only a guide and depend on the age and cut of the vegetables.

Where High power is specified in recipes, this means you are using the highest setting, full power or 100% energy output; Medium power means 50–60% and Low power 30–40%. For thawing food, use the Defrost setting. It's all very simple really. Microwave ovens are quite safe for children to use and very convenient for 'singles' of all ages who may wish to cook only small amounts of food.

Measuring Honey. *Honey is easy to measure when it is slightly liquefied. Place an opened honey jar in a microwave and microwave for a few seconds to liquefy.*

Mushroom Risotto (p. 28) served with a salad. Use a cheese slicer or sharp vegetable peeler to make shavings of Parmesan cheese to serve with the risotto.

Preparation of ingredients for Mushroom Risotto. For the best flavour, use a homemade chicken or vegetable stock if you can. Otherwise, a good commercial one will do.

Mushroom Risotto

While arborio rice grown in the Po Valley in Italy undoubtedly makes the creamiest risotto, long-grain white rice is a good substitute. If desired, a little extra butter can be stirred into the risotto just before serving. At no stage should the risotto be covered during microwaving.

1 tablespoon olive oil
60 g/2 oz/¼ cup butter
1 large onion, finely chopped
200 g/7 oz/1 cup arborio rice
200 g/7 oz/3 cups sliced button mushrooms
600 ml/1 pint/2½ cups vegetable or chicken stock

125 ml/4 fl oz/½ cup dry white wine
½ teaspoon salt
Pepper
Parsley, to garnish
Shavings of Parmesan cheese, to serve

Microwave the oil and butter in a large, deep microwave-safe dish of 2 litre/3½ pint/2¼ quart capacity on High for 1½ minutes. Add the onion and cook for 4 minutes. Stir in the rice and

Making Risotto in the Microwave

Add the chopped onion to melted oil and butter in a large bowl.

Stir in the rice and mushrooms until they glisten.

Add stock, wine and seasonings and stir.

Stir parsley through the cooked rice and fluff it up.

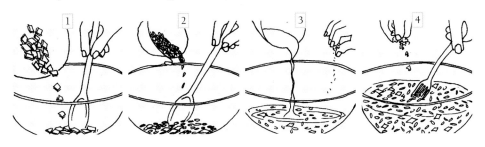

mushrooms until the rice glistens and cook for 4 minutes. Add the stock, wine, salt and pepper and stir well. Cook for 10 minutes. Stir again and cook for a further 10 minutes. Leave the risotto to stand for 5 minutes. Stir in the parsley using a fork to flake the rice. The rice should be firm in texture, *al dente*, but tender. Serve risotto with shavings of Parmesan cheese.

Serves 4 as an entrée, 2 as a main course

Vegetable Stock

This stock (or broth) is fat-free and light in flavour, so it's useful for a variety of recipes. While you can use almost any vegetables in a stock, some are more suitable than others. For example, a combination of carrots, celery, leeks and swede (rutabaga) gives a good clean vegetable flavour and clear appearance to the stock while potatoes, parsnips and pumpkin are likely to cloud the liquid. Ripe tomatoes will add colour and extra flavour, and sliced button mushrooms add yet another dimension. Avoid strongly flavoured vegetables like cabbage or broccoli. Suitable herbs to add to a vegetable stock are parsley stalks, thyme and bay leaves.

3 carrots, chopped
3 leeks, sliced
3 celery sticks, chopped
1 yellow swede (rutabaga), chopped
1 tomato

Chopped stalks from button mushrooms
6 parsley stalks
½ teaspoon black peppercorns
1 bay leaf
2 litres/3½ pints/2¼ quarts cold water

Place all the ingredients in a large pan and simmer for 1 hour. Leave to cool, then strain the stock and discard the vegetables. Chill the stock or freeze for up to six months.

Makes about 1 litre /1¾ pints/4¼ cups.

Baby Vegetables with Lemon Mousse Sauce

New season baby vegetables are delicious when served with this sunny-coloured, light lemon sauce. The sauce can be prepared a day in advance, then served with freshly cooked vegetables, cooled to room temperature. This dish makes a handsome addition to any buffet table.

200 g/7 oz baby potatoes
150 g/5 oz baby French (green) beans
175 g/6 oz baby yellow squash
1 bunch asparagus
1 bunch baby carrots

LEMON MOUSSE SAUCE
125 g/4 oz/½ cup butter
3 egg yolks
3 teaspoons lemon juice
Pinch of salt
Cayenne pepper
2 egg whites

Microwave the vegetables separately until tender and drain. Refresh the beans and asparagus under cold running water to preserve their natural green colour. Melt the butter in a microwave-safe bowl on High until it bubbles, but do not allow to brown. Place the egg yolks, lemon juice, salt and cayenne in an electric blender or food processor and blend at a low speed. Pour the hot butter in a steady stream on to the egg yolk mixture. When all of the butter is added, switch off the machine. Pour the sauce into a bowl and leave to cool, stirring occasionally to prevent a skin forming. Beat the egg whites until stiff but not rocky and fold into the sauce. Cover and chill the sauce. Serve with the cooked vegetables.

Serves 4

Right: Baby Vegetables with Lemon Mousse Sauce. Select and combine any young fresh vegetables in season. Below: Ingredients for Lemon Mousse Sauce. To save time, this sauce can be made the day before.

Red Cabbage with Pears

Red cabbage has virtually the same nutrients as green, and its wonderful fuchsia colour is a bonus. If desired, serve this dish with Polenta Blinis (p. 20) and top with a dollop of thick soured cream or yoghurt.

½ red cabbage, finely shredded
60 g/2 oz/¼ cup butter
1 onion, finely chopped
125 ml/4 oz/½ cup red wine
1 tablespoon vinegar

3 teaspoons sugar
4 cloves
2 firm ripe pears, chopped
Salt and pepper

Cover the cabbage with boiling water, leave to stand for 2 minutes and drain. Melt the butter in a large microwave-safe casserole dish on High. Add the onion and cook on High for 3 minutes. Stir in the red wine, vinegar, sugar, cloves and pears. Add the cabbage and microwave on High for 10 minutes, stirring occasionally. Season with salt and pepper and leave to stand for 5 minutes before serving.

Serves 3–4

Red Lentil and Vegetable Hot Pot

Red lentils are sometimes called Continental lentils and are a good source of protein and dietary fibre. These small lentils are very convenient to use because they are quick cooking and because they don't require soaking. You merely rinse them in a sieve to remove any grit. The dish is quite moist and makes an excellent vegetarian main course to serve alone or with a tossed salad.

2 tablespoons peanut oil
1 onion, chopped
1 garlic clove, crushed
2 teaspoons curry powder
2 teaspoons cumin seeds
250 g/9 oz red lentils

750 ml/1¼ pints/3 cups hot vegetable stock (p. 29)
2 Granny Smith apples, chopped
125/4 oz/1 cup chopped celery
¼ cabbage, chopped
300g/10 oz/2 cups frozen peas

Place the oil in a very large microwave-safe bowl or casserole, add the onion and microwave on High for 2 minutes. Add the garlic, curry powder and cumin seeds and microwave for 1 minute. Stir in the lentils, hot stock, apple, celery and cabbage. Cover with clingfilm (plastic wrap) and microwave for 10 minutes. Stir the mixture well, add peas, cover and microwave for a further 10 minutes. Leave to stand for 5 minutes before serving.

Serves 4–6

Stuffed Vegetables

Stuffed vegetables are easy to prepare and can be nutritious and inviting. While the original shape of the vegetable is preserved, the filling or stuffing often contains a surprise in the form of a complementary flavour or an unusual texture. Stuffed tomatoes and mushrooms require minimal preparation and peppers (capsicums, bell peppers) and courgettes (baby marrows, zucchini) only need blanching before stuffing. While stuffed and baked potatoes and pumpkin take a considerable time to cook, a microwave oven can cut this time by about half.

Blue Cheese Potatoes

Potatoes in their skins, baked whole in the oven or microwaved, are more nutritious than when cooked any other way. Contrary to popular belief, potatoes themselves are not fattening. It's the butter and cream we add that account for extra calories (kilojoules). To save time, the potatoes can be microwaved on High for 15 minutes, or until tender. The time needed depends on their size.

4 large potatoes	¼ cup finely chopped celery
125g/4 oz creamy blue cheese	Cracked pepper
1 tablespoon finely chopped red pepper (capsicum,	1 tablespoon chopped chives
bell pepper)	30 g/1 oz/¼ cup chopped walnuts

Scrub the potatoes well under running water and dry with a towel. Prick the skins in several places to prevent them from splitting during cooking. Brush with oil and if desired sprinkle lightly with salt. Place the potatoes on the shelf (rack) of a preheated oven and bake at 180°C/350°F/gas 4 for 1 hour, or until tender when pierced with a skewer. Cut a slice from the top of each potato and carefully remove the flesh, leaving quite a thick potato wall. Mash the hot potato flesh lightly, add the cheese, pepper, celery and cracked pepper. Pile the potato mixture back into the shells, and top with the chives and walnuts. Reheat potatoes for a few minutes before serving.

Serves 4

Chèvre (Fresh Goat's Cheese). *Can be substituted for blue cheese in this recipe. Use goat's cheese without the traditional ash coating.*

Mini Pumpkins with Fruity Couscous

Couscous is regarded as the national dish of Morocco. Tiny cream-coloured couscous pellets are made from semolina, moistened and coated with flour. They in fact contain more protein than rice, rye or wheat. Now available in convenient instant form, couscous cooks or steams in minutes and today it can be found on the menus of many top restaurants. Pine nuts are the delicious seeds of the Mediterranean stone pine tree and an essential ingredient in pesto, Italy's fragrant basil sauce. To toast pine nuts, place them in a dry pan and stir continuously over a moderate heat until golden. Remove to a plate to cool.

4 golden nugget pumpkins
30 g/1 oz/2 tablespoons butter
1 tablespoon currants
30 g/1 oz/¼ cup chopped dried apricots
125 g/4 oz/1 cup couscous

½ teaspoon ground cumin
175 ml/6 fl oz/¾ cup hot vegetable stock (p, 29)
2 tablespoons toasted pine nuts
Coriander (cilantro), to garnish

Cut the tops off the pumpkins and scoop out the seeds and soft membrane. Put 1 teaspoon of water inside each pumpkin and place the pumpkins on a microwave-safe plate. Cover with microwave-safe clingfilm (plastic wrap) and microwave on High for about 15 minutes, until the pumpkins are tender when tested with a skewer. (The pumpkins may also be baked in a pre-heated oven at 190°C/375°F/gas 5 for about 45 minutes, or until tender when tested.) Melt the butter in a pan, add the currants, apricots and couscous and stir over a low heat for a minute. Add the cumin and vegetable stock. Bring the mixture to the boil, remove from the heat, cover and leave to stand for 3 minutes. Stir the pine nuts into the couscous with a fork, and spoon the mixture into the hot cooked pumpkins. Serve garnished with coriander.

Serves 4

Keeping Coriander (Cilantro) Fresh. *To keep a bunch of coriander fresh for longer, place upright in a jug of water. Cover the exposed leaves with a polythene bag and chill, changing the water daily.*

Hollowing Out Mini Pumpkins

Cut the tops off the pumpkins.	*Cut neatly around the ridge of the pumpkin between the flesh and the seeds.*	*Cut a cross on the top of the soft membrane containing the seeds.*	*Scoop out the seeds with a serrated spoon.*

Mini Pumpkins with Fruity Couscous. It is a delight to prepare these beautifully coloured pumpkins with a savoury filling. They look very attractive when served.

Bean-Filled Peppers

Freshly cooked or canned cannelini beans can be used in this recipe.

2 large peppers (capsicums, bell peppers)
2 tablespoons olive oil
1 onion, chopped
1 garlic clove, crushed
75 g/2½ oz/1 cup sliced button mushrooms

2 tomatoes, peeled seeded and chopped
1 tablespoon chopped oregano
400 g/14 oz/2 cups cooked cannelini (butter) beans
(p. 13)
Salt and pepper

Cut the peppers in half lengthwise, remove the membrane and seeds, keeping the shells intact. Drop the peppers into boiling water and cook for 3 minutes. Drain and refresh under cold running water. Heat the oil in a pan, add the onion and garlic and cook gently until the onion is soft. Add the mushrooms, tomato, oregano, beans, salt and pepper. Pile the bean mixture in to the peppers. Place the peppers in a shallow ovenproof dish and cover with foil. Bake in a preheated oven at 180°C/350°F/gas 4 for about 25 minutes, until peppers are tender.
Serves 4

Step by Step

Baking

The aroma and flavour of foods cooked in the oven are very enticing. Cooking vegetables this way helps to preserve valuable nutrients as little if any water is used. Dry heat will crisp the skin of hard vegetables such as pumpkin and potatoes and oven-cooking brings out the natural sugar content of parsnips, leeks and peppers, making them truly delicious.

Baked Ricottas with Fresh Tomato Sauce

Soft, creamy ricotta cheese is made from the whey of separated cow's or sheep's milk and is low in fat. These fragrant baked ricottas make an excellent starter for a meal.

2 courgettes (baby marrows, zucchini)
450 g/1 lb ricotta cheese
Finely grated peel of ½ lemon
1 small garlic clove, crushed

¼ teaspoon cracked pepper
4 teaspoons virgin olive oil

Fresh Tomato Sauce, to serve (p. 14)

Baked Ricottas with Fresh Tomato Sauce. The courgette (baby marrow, zucchini) strips ready to blanch for lining the moulds.

Baked Ricottas with Fresh Tomato Sauce may be served warm or they can be prepared the day before and allowed to come to room temperature before serving.

Peel strips from the courgettes lengthwise, using a vegetable peeler. Place the strips in a heat-proof bowl, cover with boiling water and leave to stand for 30 seconds. Drain and rinse under cold water, pat the strips dry with paper towels. Brush four 250 ml/8 fl oz/1 cup capacity moulds with oil and make a cross with two courgette strips in each mould, trimming the edges if necessary. Mix the ricotta, lemon peel, garlic and pepper together and divide the mixture between the moulds, packing down firmly. Drizzle a teaspoon of olive oil on top of each mould. Bake the moulds, uncovered, in a preheated oven at 190°C/375°F/gas 5 for about 20 minutes, until the ricotta is firm. Invert on to serving plates and serve with the fresh tomato sauce.

Serves 4

Mediterranean Baked Vegetables

Take a variety of brightly coloured vegetables and anoint them with an olive oil and herb mixture. Bake them until tender when they will be surprisingly aromatic, then drizzle a few drops of rich, mellow Balsamic vinegar over them. Surprisingly simple, yet so delicious!

4 baby aubergines (eggplants)	2 garlic cloves, crushed
Salt	3 tablespoons virgin olive oil
4 courgettes (baby marrows, zucchini)	1 teaspoon caster (superfine) sugar
4 yellow baby squash	1 tablespoon chopped thyme
4 egg tomatoes	2 tablespoons balsamic vinegar
2 red and 2 green peppers (capsicums, bell peppers)	Crusty bread, to serve

Cut the aubergines and courgettes in half, score the cut surfaces and sprinkle with salt. Leave to stand for 15 minutes, then pat dry with paper towels. Trim the baby squash. Cut a shallow cross in each tomato, cut the peppers into quarters and remove the seeds. Arrange the vegetables in a single layer in an ovenproof dish. Mix the garlic, olive oil, sugar and thyme and drizzle over the vegetables. Bake in a preheated oven at 180C°/ 350°F/gas 4, uncovered, for about 30 minutes. Sprinkle the balsamic vinegar over the vegetables and serve with crusty bread.

Serves 4

Roasted Red Peppers

Sometimes peppers have a harsh flavour and seem difficult to digest. However, when roasted and skinned, their flavour is far sweeter, their texture more delicious and succulent and digestion problems magically disappear. Roasted red peppers have a wonderful flavour and can be used in many recipes. You can also grill (broil) peppers, following the recipe for roasting.

Red peppers (capsicums, bell peppers)	Light olive oil

Cut the peppers in half lengthwise and remove the membrane and seeds. Place on a baking sheet in a single layer and brush the peppers lightly with oil. Bake in a preheated oven at 180°C/ 350°F/gas 4 for about 30 minutes, until the skin blisters. (Take care not to allow peppers to scorch.) Remove from the baking sheet and place the peppers in a polythene bag, folding the end of the bag underneath. Leave the peppers to stand for 10 minutes to steam, after which they will peel easily.

Fresh from the oven, Mediterranean Baked Vegetables are delicious served with crusty bread and a glass or two of wine.

Carrot and Walnut Muffins

So quick and easy to make, these muffins are perfect for packing in a lunch box or serving with a bowl of steaming homemade soup.

175 g/6 oz/1½ cups self-raising (self-rising) flour
½ teaspoon salt
125 g/4 oz/1 cup grated Cheddar cheese
30 g/1 oz/¼ cup chopped walnuts
125 g/4 oz/1 cup grated carrot

1 tablespoon snipped chives
1 egg
3 tablespoons vegetable or light olive oil
175 ml/6 fl oz/¾ cup milk

Sift the flour and salt into a bowl. Add the cheese, walnuts, carrot and chives. Beat the egg, oil and milk together and add to the dry ingredients, stirring to make a thick batter. Fill well-greased bun tins (muffin pans) three-quarters full with the mixture. Bake in a preheated oven at 200°C/400°F/gas 6 for 20–25 minutes.
Makes about 12

Potato, Leek and Olive Pie

This easy potato pie evokes memories of the Mediterranean with ingredients such as virgin olive oil, ripe olives, aromatic thyme and Parmesan cheese. Potatoes, nutritious at any time, are an even better source of dietary fibre if cooked in their skins.

2 tablespoons virgin olive oil
2 leeks, sliced finely
750 g/1¾ lb potatoes, unpeeled
75 g/2½ oz/½ cup sliced black olives

1 tablespoon chopped thyme
125 g/4 oz/1 cup grated Cheddar cheese
Salt and pepper
30 g/1 oz/¼ cup grated Parmesan cheese

Heat the oil in a pan and cook the leeks over a low heat for 10 minutes, stirring occasionally. Do not allow them to brown. Cut the potatoes into 6 mm/¼ inch slices. Arrange layers of the potatoes with leeks, olives, thyme, Cheddar cheese, salt and pepper in a buttered 23 cm/9 inch shallow pie dish, finishing with a layer of potatoes. Sprinkle with the Parmesan cheese. Cover the dish loosely with foil and bake in a preheated oven at 200°C/400°F/gas 6 for about 50 minutes. Remove the foil and bake a further 15 minutes or until the top is golden brown.
Serves 6

Carrot and Walnut Muffins are equally good with coffee or tea. Serve them piping hot, spread with polyunsaturated margarine, or butter if you prefer.

Put the pastry ball on a floured board.

Knead until smooth and chill for 30 minutes.

Roll out pastry and put a quarter of it over a tartlet tin (pan).

Press the pastry in, roll over the top of tin to cut off excess pastry.

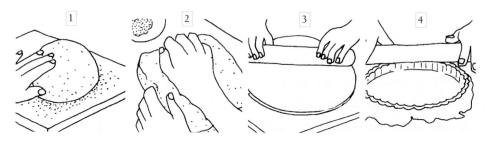

Goat's Cheese and Sun-Dried Tomato Tartlets

For this recipe use a soft creamy fresh goat's cheese (chèvre), which has no dark ash coating. Sun-dried tomatoes have a wonderfully intense tomato flavour and are generally sold packed in olive oil. You can either make tartlets or make one larger tart as shown on page two. Use a tart tin 18 cm (7 inch) in diameter and bake for a further 10 minutes.

FOOD PROCESSOR PASTRY (PIE DOUGH)
125 g/4 oz/1 cup plain (all-purpose) flour
2 tablespoons grated Parmesan cheese
Pinch of salt
60 g/2 oz/¼ cup chilled butter, diced
2 egg yolks
1 tablespoon iced water

FILLING
2 eggs
125 ml/4fl oz/½ cup cream
1 tablespoon chopped basil
2 teaspoons snipped chives
Salt and pepper
125 g/4 oz fresh goat's cheese (chèvre), chopped
30 g/1 oz/¼ cup chopped sun-dried tomatoes

To make the pastry, blend the flour, Parmesan and salt in a food processor for a few seconds until combined. Add the diced butter and process until the mixture resembles breadcrumbs. Beat the egg yolks and iced water together and pour over the dry ingredients. Process rapidly, but stop when the dough starts to form the ball around the blade. Turn dough on to a board, knead only until smooth and wrap in clingfilm (plastic wrap). Chill the pastry for 30 minutes only. Roll the pastry out to fit four 10 cm/4 inch tartlet tins (pans) and prick in several places. Bake in a preheated oven at 190°C/375°F/gas 5 for 10 minutes. Meanwhile, prepare the filling.

To make the filling, beat the eggs lightly in a bowl and stir in the cream, basil, chives, salt and pepper. Scatter the chèvre and the sun-dried tomatoes into the hot pastry cases. Spoon the egg mixture on top, ensuring tomatoes are covered. Bake the tartlets for a further 15 minutes until lightly set.

Serves 4

Egg Dishes

Apart from providing essential protein to vegetable recipes, eggs contribute a variety of welcome textures to dishes. They can make a delicious, super-light soufflé, an impressive roulade or a nourishing frittata or omelette. Eggs can be used to set a vegetable mixture or bind a stuffing. They also make a nutritious, colourful garnish for vegetable dishes. When preparing hard-boiled eggs for garnish, use eggs that are a few days old as newly laid eggs are generally difficult to peel. Ensure that eggs are at room temperature before cooking. If eggs are cold they will crack when they are put into boiling water. For an attractive garnish for cooked leeks, beans and asparagus, separate the yolks from the whites of hard-boiled eggs, rinse the whites, pat dry and chop finely. Sieve the yolks and arrange a row of whites and yolks over cooked vegetables.

Herb Roulade with Roasted Peppers (p. 44). Here is the roulade ready for rolling, using a tea-towel (dish cloth) as a guide. The roulade filling consists of ricotta cheese scattered with colourful roasted peppers(capsicums, bell peppers), black olives and basil.

Herb Roulade with Roasted Peppers

A roulade mixture is similar to a soufflé mixture but differs in that it is baked in a Swiss roll (jelly roll) tin, and is then filled with an interesting mixture and rolled up. Depending on the type of filling used, a roulade may be served hot or cold, although this recipe should be served at room temperature. It can be prepared a day in advance and makes an attractive starter or light luncheon dish.

ROULADE
60 g/2 oz/¼ cup butter
45 g/1½ oz/⅓ cup plain (all-purpose) flour
250 ml/8 fl oz/1 cup milk
4 eggs, separated
1 tablespoon chopped parsley
1 tablespoon snipped chives

Salt and pepper

FILLING
375 g/13 oz/1⅔ cups ricotta cheese
2 roasted peppers, (capsicums, bell peppers),
   chopped (p. 39)
45 g/1½ oz/¼ cup sliced black olives
1 tablespoon chopped basil

Line a 25 x 30 cm/1O x 12 inch Swiss roll (jelly roll) tin with foil or non-stick (baker's) parchment and grease lightly. Melt the butter in a pan and remove from the heat. Stir in the flour and blend in the milk. Return the pan to the heat and stir continuously until the mixture boils and thickens. Simmer for 1 minute. Remove the pan from the heat and stir in the egg yolks, herbs, salt and pepper. Beat the herb mixture. Pour into the prepared pan, spreading the mixture gently and evenly. Bake in a preheated oven at 220° C/425° F/gas 7 for about 15 minutes, until well-risen and golden brown. Turn out on to a wire rack lined with a tea-towel (dish cloth). Remove the paper carefully and leave the roulade to cool. Beat the ricotta cheese until smooth and spread gently over the roulade. Scatter the peppers, olives and basil over the cheese. Roll the roulade and serve at room temperature.

Serves 6

Rolling the Roulade. *The most difficult thing about the making of a roulade is the rolling procedure. However, this is easily done if you commence rolling from the far side, bringing the roulade towards you. Use the paper as a guide when rolling.*

An individual serving of Herb Roulade with Roasted Peppers. The savoury filling of roasted peppers (capsicums, bell peppers), black olives and basil enhances the soufflé and risotto base.

Twice-Baked Spinach Soufflés

The thought of making soufflés terrifies some people–unjustifiably. Soufflés are easy and make an impressive entrée at a dinner party. This recipe can be prepared the day before and chilled after the first baking. Although these soufflés will collapse after the first baking, don't be alarmed. With a little further treatment and a second baking they rise beautifully. Once you have mastered the art, you'll serve them often as they are spectacular and delicious.

Grated nutmeg

45 g/1½ oz/⅓ cup plain (all-purpose) flour

5 egg whites

250 ml/8 fl oz/1 cup milk

150 ml/¼ pint/⅔ cup double (heavy) cream

½ cup finely chopped cooked leaf spinach

60 g/2 oz/½ cup grated Gruyère cheese

4 egg yolks

60 g/2 oz/½ cup grated Parmesan cheese

Salt and pepper

Butter six soufflé moulds of about 250 ml/8 fl oz/1 cup capacity generously and place a circle of greased foil in the base of each mould. Melt the butter in a large pan and remove from the heat. Stir in the flour and blend in the milk. Return the pan to the heat and stir continuously until the mixture boils and thickens. Simmer for 1 minute. Remove the pan from the heat and stir in the spinach, egg yolks, salt, pepper and nutmeg. Beat the egg whites in a bowl until stiff but not rocky and fold into the mixture. Spoon into the moulds. Bake soufflés in a *bain marie* at 200°C/400°F/gas 6 for about 22 minutes, until well-risen and cooked. Allow soufflés to cool. Unmould the soufflés carefully into buttered gratin dishes and remove the foil. Spread the cream evenly over the soufflés, scatter the combined cheeses on top and bake at the same temperature for 12 minutes or until the soufflés are puffed and golden. Serve immediately.

Serves 6

Twice-Baked Spinach Soufflés

| Prepare soufflé moulds with butter and a circle of foil. | Mix soufflé mixture together in pan and fold in the egg whites. | Pour mixture into the moulds. | Bake until well-risen and cooked. |

Cooking Spinach. *To cook the spinach for this recipe in a microwave, remove the stems, wash the spinach thoroughly, shaking the excess water away. Place on a microwave-safe plate, cover with clingfilm (plastic wrap) and microwave until cooked. Plunge the spinach into cold water. Drain by pressing firmly between two plates which are then tilted to allow water to escape.*

Crustless Seakale Quiche

Seakale beet, Swiss chard or silverbeet has a broad leaf with a thick white stalk. It is related to garden beetroot and sugar beets and tastes delicious in this easy quiche without pastry. Serve the quiche warm or at room temperature, with salad or colourful vegetables. It also reheats well in a microwave oven.

60 g/2 oz/½ cup plain (all-purpose) flour
½ teaspoon baking powder
125 g/4 oz/1 cup grated Gruyère cheese
175 g/6 oz/1 cup cooked seakale (Swiss chard,
  silverbeet), well-drained and chopped

45 g/1½ oz/¼ cup chopped spring onions (scallions)
4 eggs
350 ml/12 fl oz/1½ cups milk
60 g/2 oz/¼ cup butter, melted
Salt and pepper

Sift the flour and baking powder into a large bowl and add the cheese, seakale and spring onions. Beat the eggs lightly in a separate bowl and add the milk, butter, salt and pepper. Combine the two mixtures and pour into a well-buttered 23 cm/9 inch quiche dish. Bake in a preheated oven at 190°C/375°F/gas 5 for about 35 minutes, until lightly set.
Serves 6

Broccoli Frittata

The broccoli for this recipe can be easily cooked in a microwave. Trim the stalks close to the broccoli florets. Cut 2 cm/1 inch florets and place on a microwave-safe plate, sprinkle with a tablespoon of water, cover with cling film (plastic wrap) and microwave on High for about 2 minutes. Rinse under cold water and drain well.

8 eggs
125 g/4 oz/1 cup grated Gruyère cheese
4 green shallots, sliced
150 g/5 oz/2 cups broccoli florets, cooked

Salt and pepper
Freshly ground pepper
2 tablespoons olive oil
30 g/1 oz/¼ cup grated Parmesan cheese

Beat the eggs lightly in a bowl. Add the Gruyère cheese, shallots and broccoli and season with salt and pepper. Heat the oil in a large heavy frying pan (skillet) and pour in the egg mixture. Cook over a gentle heat, lifting the edges to allow the uncooked egg mixture to run underneath. When the bottom of the frittata appears cooked and the top is lightly set, sprinkle with the Parmesan and grill (broil) until the cheese is golden.
Serves 4

Glossary

Bain marie A container partly filled with water. A dish of food placed in a *bain marie* will not cook too quickly in the oven. It can also be used to keep food warm.

Bake 'blind' To partially bake an unfilled pastry case. The pastry is lined with foil or non-stick (baker's) parchment and filled with rice, beans or pastry weights for this procedure.

Balsamic vinegar See page 11.

Bind To add an egg or liquid to a food mixture to hold it together.

Blanch To immerse food briefly in boiling water to soften it or remove skin.

Blini A pancake made with yeast.

Cèpes, porcini and morels Wild mushrooms commonly marketed as dried mushrooms. They need to be soaked in water to soften before cooking.

Marinade Liquid used for marinating, usually wine, oil, vinegar, lemon juice, herbs and spices.

Marinate To soak raw ingredients in a liquid to preserve them and make them more tender.

Microwave-safe container A heatproof, non-metal container suitable for use in a microwave oven.

Preheated oven One that has reached the desired temperature by the time you need to use it. Most ovens will take about 15 minutes to heat to the required temperature.

Refresh To place blanched foods under cold running water to cool them quickly, to prevent further cooking and preserve their natural colour.

Shallots A member of the onion family; shallots are smaller than onions and more delicate tasting. Substitute spring onions (scallions or green onions).

Simmer To keep a liquid just below boiling point so that it 'shivers'.

Skim To remove the scum from a liquid after it comes to the boil, usually with a large spoon or a flat sieve (strainer).

Sweat To soften vegetables by cooking them gently in butter or oil until they release their juices but do not brown.

Vinaigrette A clear dressing made from 4 parts oil to 1 part vinegar.

Vinegar Produced by acetic fermentation of wine or cider. It can be flavoured by herbs, spices, shallots and garlic or raspberries.

Wire rack For cooling cakes and biscuits (cookies).